The Dangers of Living with

a Drug Addict

and how to Stay Safe.

Vivienne Gardner Edwards

For Dana
Thank you for everything.
I learned so much from you.
Also,
With grateful thanks to the hundreds of families
who have shared their struggles with me. They have
all contributed to this book.

Contents

Living with a Drug Addict

Living with a drug addict brings up many different safety issues. I know that if you are not an addict, you may think that the drug use cannot hurt you. I thought that, but I was so wrong.

After years of dealing with my business partner who was also my housemate and friend, and putting up with the dangers associated with her drug use, plus dealing with her abuse and violence, I am much more aware of safety issues than I ever thought about before.

I want to share some of these with you so you can learn from my mistakes. Not everything will apply to your situation, but take what is useful and never think for a moment that this could not happen to you.

To begin with, I did not know that she (I'll call her Jeanette) was back to using drugs. I did know that she had been a user, actually a heavy user, for some years. Her drugs of choice were methamphetamine and marijuana. I knew a little about the effects of marijuana but next to nothing about meth.

I had no direct experience of any drug use as I have never used drugs or even smoked cigarettes. I had no idea what signs to look for and as I cared about her and our business, I trusted her. Big mistake, as I then learned the hard way!

We began sharing a home after my divorce. She talked quite openly about her previous drug use but she had been to a rehab at least twice. She appeared clean and held down a job. She also gave up smoking when I told her I could not stand living with secondhand smoke. None of these things lasted long.

When you have a family member who is using any kind of drug, it is a mind altering substance. Therefore, that person does not operate in the same way that non-drug users do. At the time I did not understand the long-term damage that some drugs can do.

I later learned that many drug users began using drugs to 'self-medicate', because the drug makes them feel better or more normal or more able to work or just cope with life. This is quite often due to an underlying or undiagnosed mental condition, so they self medicate rather than a visit to a doctor. Whatever started the user down the path, the result is that you are probably dealing with someone who was originally not functioning very well mentally, and the drug use makes things much worse.

This can actually be an understatement, as I found out after just a few months with Jeanette. I know that Jeanette had untreated ADHD (attention deficit hyperactivity disorder) so I believe this was a contributing factor when she started using drugs in her teens. I believe it is quite possible that most drug users have some kind of mental unbalance. Even if they did not have a problem before their drug use, they certainly end up with one from the effects of drugs. The symptoms of this imbalance can range from the occasional pot smoker who is being a bit 'out-of-it' to a full blown meth addict who has reached the 'tweaker' stage.

A Tweaker? What's that?

The term tweaker refers to a methamphetamine user. Actually, a heavy meth user, and this is what happens. After a certain quantity of the drug has been used over a number of hours or days, the user can no longer get high from the drug. They have often been awake for days - sometimes as long as fifteen days in a row with no sleep - and they become delusional. They are in a living hell of their own doing. They want to sleep but they cannot. They want to feel a high from the drug but they cannot. They want someone to help them but they reject all offers of help. They become paranoid, suspicious, unreasonable and angry.

Tweakers are very dangerous people. Never trust anyone who shows signs of being at this stage. They can travel from apathy to murderous rage in a split second. If the user in your household is using meth, be very watchful. Meth use often increases and increases to the point of tweaking. These tweakers are at the end of a methamphetamine binge.

They may talk to themselves, or shout, mutter and gesture.

They will talk at 100 miles an hour and hallucinations are common.

They may wander into traffic or into other unsafe situations.

They think everyone is out to get them, and may become deeply suspicious of any offers of help.

Any sudden movement may be interpreted as a threat and they may attack you without warning.

They may twitch and jerk or they may lapse into an apathetic state.

Check out their eyes because they will probably be doing some twitching and jerking.

They may appear rational one minute and the next be rambling in a world of their own.

Tweakers also fiddle with things in an endless pattern. They may take things apart - things which they have no hope of ever being able to put back together. They may pick endlessly at their skin. I have watched Jeanette pick at her face for a full hour and a half. They might mindlessly sort things - anything from papers, to rocks to car parts.

Sometimes they think they have bugs under their skin and have even been known to take a blade and try and cut them out. They will often act on impulse and go shoplifting or purse snatching. They can display very irrational behavior. Above all they can erupt into violent rage over anything or nothing. Anyone who gets in their way can get hurt.

Never try and confront someone if you think they are at this stage. They are far too dangerous and you cannot reason with them. If you know that the drug user in your family is on meth, please be very careful. Any action you take may alarm someone who is at the stage of tweaking. They will be suspicious of everything and everyone. If I had known more about the effects of meth when dealing with Jeanette, I would not have made the mistakes I did.

However, if you are absolutely forced to deal with someone who you think is at the tweaking stage, there are some important things to remember.

Speak slowly and clearly.

Do not raise your voice or appear angry.

Do not confront them about their drug use or anything else.

Do not make any sudden movements.

Keep your hands where they can be seen.

Do not pick up anything that may be considered a weapon.

Do not use any bright lights.

Stay calm but watchful.

If you feel unsafe then you probably are. Do not hesitate to leave and then call the police. Let them know that the person may be high on meth. They are used to dealing with these people.

In my opinion, methamphetamine is one of the most dangerous of all drugs. It is fairly cheap, easy to find, easy to make, can be used in a number of ways, and it makes life hell for the people who are around a user. If your family member uses meth, please make sure you have an escape plan ready and do not be afraid to use it. See information later in this book for how to make a plan.

Whatever drug the person in your home is using, there is still serious potential for all kinds of dangers in your home.

Children's Safety.

If you have children in the home, the chances are that any drug use is going to adversely affect them. This is a huge issue so please take this seriously. You may not find out for years that your child was sexually assaulted by the drug user's friends, but it can and does happen. One local drug user known to me actually traded her small child for dope. Another woman known to me traded her small son to a man in exchange for a car and money. Yes, that is how sick these people can be.

Now is the time to talk with your children about what is appropriate for people to do to them. Explain about touching and describe good touch and bad touch. Include hitting and slapping in the bad touch as well. It is possible for children to be physically abused in your absence. To deal with inappropriate sexual touching, the best way is to tell them that any part of their body that would be covered by a swim suit is their private area, and not to be touched by anyone. This, of course, should be a part of your whole system of educating them about what is OK for anyone to do to them, adults or even other children.

If you are not totally comfortable with talking to your children about sexual touching then there are a number of good books written for children. Doing a search on Amazon under children's books brings up several for different ages. Also the librarian at your local library would be able to suggest suitable books. This is a great way to reinforce what you have been teaching.

Statistics show that most children are sexually touched or molested by a person known to them. In the case of people coming to the house to see the addict, they may be named as Uncles or Aunts, thus giving the children a family association. When you talk to your children, make sure that they know that they are safe to come to you with questions or to tell you if something bothers them.

If the addict has a lot of time alone with the children, be doubly careful. Not only can they be abused by the addict or their friends, but can be drawn into the drug use too. One mother I dealt with had come home from work early to find her seven and five year olds watching daddy snort cocaine from the coffee table. She had not heard what he was doing because he told the children it was their secret. This is a good time to explain that some adults may do things that are not right and then want it to be a secret. Children need to know it is OK to tell this type of 'secret'.

Another issue to be aware of is pornography. This is another one of those nasty hidden issues that no one is willing to talk about. In recent months more and more information is coming out in the media about child pornography and there are huge networks of pedophiles who are willing to pay a lot of money for photographs of children naked or in suggestive positions.

Again, if your children are alone with the drug user, gently ask if anyone takes pictures of them while you are gone. Remembering that addicts have to find money for their habit, so selling pornographic photos of children is a way to bring in cash. More than one family has discovered that even though their child was not sexually touched, Uncle Jake came with his camera and took lots of photos of the kids naked. Do you want to consider that photos of your child are being passed around on child porn sites or Facebook?

There is another situation that may be risky and that is where even though the drug user does not live with you, he/she still has your children for any unsupervised time. If you know or suspect that this person is a drug user, double your efforts to make sure they are not being molested or photographed.

Some years ago I had a disturbing conversation with the principal of our local grade school. He told me that a number of the children in school could accurately describe loading a crack pipe and explain how it is smoked. The bottom line here is that if you have children in the same house as an addict, be very careful and very watchful. They may well be learning things you would rather they did not know, and they may not tell you about visitors, secrets or photographs unless you ask.

Fire.

Jeanette set fire to the sofa on our front porch. It was only by the grace of God that the house did not burn down. It appears she lit a pipe and then forgot about it. The foam sofa cushions must have smoldered for hours before she saw what was happening. After she got the fire out, she turned the cushions over and covered the sofa with a blanket so that I would not see what she had done.

Cigarettes and pipes can easily be left burning where they can start a fire. Looking back, I am very surprised that she never managed to really burn the house down. Actually, any electric appliance can be misused; pans can be left on a stove with the burner on full; heaters can be covered with curtains or clothing and catch fire.

Propane torches are often used to smoke crystal meth or crack cocaine, and they can also start a fire or explode if heated. Liquids that are 'huffed', and the rags they are soaked in, can cause fires. See the next section on paraphernalia for more on solvents. I removed all the candles from the house after the kitchen cabinets got burned when a lighted candle underneath them caught the wood.

Drug users very often do not notice the smell of smoke or fumes, and no matter what drug is used, they affect memory, especially short-term memory. This means that the user will not remember the pipe left burning, the candles, the pan on the stove or the bonfire in the backyard.

For your safety, be sure you have adequate smoke detectors in your home and test them regularly. Also have at least one fire extinguisher, and two would be better. Remember to check them when you check your smoke detector batteries to be sure they are holding their charge.

If there should be a fire, do not expect the drug user to be of much help. Emergencies are not their thing. It is unlikely that they will find the fire extinguisher, call 911 or grab the baby or the cat.

Be sure your children know how to respond to any fire or smoke. I made it a game with my kids, when they were small, so that they knew what to do in bad situations like a fire. There is some good information on fire safety for children at the website of the US Fire Administration. There is also a neat coloring book you can download and some fun fire quizzes. See http://www.usfa.fema.gov/kids/

Drug paraphernalia

Another huge danger in the home can be from drug paraphernalia which may be left around the house. Lighters, razor blades, drug residue, used syringes or questionable liquids in small bottles; all of these pose a threat to anyone who does not recognize them or who suddenly gets stuck with an infected needle. This is particularly dangerous for children who like to explore things and who also put anything and everything into their mouth. If there is drug residue on any surface, the children are vulnerable as they can pick up drugs from a surface and transfer it to their mouth or eyes.

It is common for cocaine or meth users to crush and snort the drug on a counter or coffee table. Residue can easily be picked up by anyone and ingested. If the user is into huffing, or inhaling fumes from any type of solvent to get high, it is often done from a rag soaked in the liquid. These rags can cause a fire. Spontaneous combustion is quite possible, especially if the rags are hidden in a small space. Heat will build up and they will ignite.

Some of the more common things used for huffing are gasoline, paint thinners, cleaning fluids, acetone (nail polish remover) or glue. Of course as well as being a fire danger, the user can die from sudden cardiac arrest.

Pills in any form can be extremely dangerous not only for small children but also pets. Jeanette dropped pills all the time and I had to keep a careful watch to see that the dogs were not able to pick them up.

As I mentioned above, a stick from a used needle can be serious. They can be contaminated with anything the user has, and many serious illnesses are blood borne, with HIV and Hepatitis being the most common.

Chunks of drugs are often cut up with bare razor blades. Severe cuts can result if you touch one or, as I did, step on one in the bathroom with bare feet.

Many drug users take kitchen equipment to use for their drugs so anything may be contaminated with residue or blood. Straws are used for snorting, and snorting often causes nose bleeds. Straws with traces of the user's blood or drug residue are not something you or your children would want to use for your soda.

Glass pipes are used for smoking crack cocaine or crystal meth. These pipes can break and I have seen the bits of a broken glass pipe hidden down the side of a chair. Nasty if you put you hand down there. Glass pipes are often hidden in car seats. Small fingers might find them there too.

Even as I write this, more drugs are appearing on the streets and in so many different forms. Also drug users are finding many different ways to use these drugs. Drug paraphernalia is no longer limited to pipes, bongs and mirrors but can encompass so may every day items. If you find any strange items, from cut up cans to stains on furniture or unknown residue on glassware, be very careful of handling these things. Some chemicals can be disastrous even in small quantities and all can be absorbed through the skin.

Accidental Drug Ingestion.

It is possible to get an accidental dose of any drug which the user has in their possession. Users are not known for their care with their belongings. Drugs can be dropped or residue spread around the living space. Contaminants from smoking crystal meth can cling to clothing and furnishings. Some drugs in liquid form such as PCP can quickly be absorbed through the skin. Drugs crushed on surfaces can be picked up and absorbed.

Drugs can also be added intentionally to drinks or food in the house. Some users think this is a joke and find it very funny to tamper with food or drinks belong to other people in the home. This can end in disaster as I have known of family members being admitted to hospital with strange symptoms. Be cautious with your food and drinks and if something appears tampered with or tastes 'off' in any way it is better to discard it than risk using it with the possible consequences. This is one time where a spy cam is very useful in the kitchen.

It is also not unknown for drug users to do this to each other and intentionally pass along nasty mixtures of drugs. Regardless of whether this is regarded as 'fun' or a get-even ploy, it is a possibility. An IV drug user known to me was given a 'hot-shot' by an acquaintance and ended up in the ICU for five days.

Infection

Another danger of a drug user in the home is infections. HIV/AIDS is common among users and so is Hepatitis C. Both of these are passed via blood, so any syringe or other equipment which has been used by the infected person is a hazard. A jab by a used syringe or needle can pass infection along immediately. Often the syringe will contain the user's blood as it is common for them to pull back on the syringe to make sure they are in a vein. Hepatitis C is pretty common among intravenous drug users. In fact over half of all drug users who inject their drugs, are infected with Hep C. As it is passed in blood it is possible to pass this infection during sexual activity.

Symptoms of Hep C infection can be vague, with fatigue, joint or muscle pains, stomach pain and nausea or loss of appetite. As you can see, these things may also have many other causes. If you know the user in your house regularly injects their drug, it might be a good idea to consult your doctor about getting tested for Hep C.

Drug users can get infected sores and MRSA's (pronounced 'mercer'). MRSA stands for Methicillin-Resistant Staphylococcus Aureus, which is a type of infection which is resistant to antibiotics and can be fatal. It can be responsible for serious skin and soft tissue infections and for a serious form of pneumonia. If you have any doubts about the dangers of MRSA, just Google pictures of MRSA sores. They are not pretty and can easily kill or disfigure you.

MRSA infections can be spread by the sharing of needles or any drug paraphernalia. Even using towels or a razor belonging to some with MRSA can pass the infection on. To be safe, do not share clothing or other items that may have been contaminated by sores or blood on the user. The user should be encouraged to keep any sores covered plus lots of hand washing is in order. Be very careful around any blood related issues. The user getting accidently cut can spread blood over furniture, walls, counters etc. Try not to come in contact with the blood, and when cleaning up, using a diluted bleach solution is a good idea.

Even if the user in your house does not admit to injecting drugs, remember that drug users rarely admit to others the extent of their use. You may not know what form their drug use actually takes. It can only take one time using an infected needle to pass Hep C along.

15

Once I knew that Jeanette was using drugs again, I was very careful about cleaning the bathroom and kitchen before I used either one. She was not fussy about hygiene and never cleaned anything up after she used it. Once I saw, via the spy cams, that she was snorting meth on the kitchen counter, my cleaning efforts doubled. It was the first thing I did when returning from work and after getting up in the morning.

Sexual Activity

Drug users can be irresponsible over safety in their sexual activity and often end up with sexually transmitted diseases. If you are having sexual relations with the user, you stand a good chance of getting anything that they are infected with. Condoms are some protection but are not totally adequate to be a certainty.

Chlamydia is one of the most common sexually transmitted diseases but often has few symptoms. According to the CDC, there were 1,412,791 cases of Chlamydia reported to them in 2011. Most of these were young people between the ages of 15 and 29. Sadly Chlamydia can cause infertility and infection in the fallopian tubes of women before any symptoms are noticed. It can also be passed to an unborn baby. If you are pregnant or thinking of becoming pregnant, check with your doctor to get tested for Chlamydia. It is treatable with antibiotics..

There are other STD's (Sexually Transmitted Diseases) that can be passed along including Genital Herpes, Gonorrhea, Syphilis and of course HIV/Aids. The bottom line here is that if you are having any sexual relations with the drug user, be sure to use condoms and speak with your doctor about any symptoms you notice. Oral or anal sex can still pass STD's from the drug user.

Sex is also used as an exchange for drugs. Men as well as women trade sexual acts for their drug supply. The more partners the user has, the more there is a risk of contracting a disease.

Even if the drug user has been tested for any sexually transmitted infection and assuming that you have proof that the tests were negative, there is still the issue of infection occurring after the testing was done. This means that just because your partner was infection free three months ago does not necessarily mean that they are infection free today.

Visitors.

Have you ever had a strange man just open the door and walk into your home? I have, and I was more shocked than I can say when I realized that he walked in to find Jeanette. Obviously he had no idea I was there, and was apparently used to just walking in when he felt like it. He left faster than he entered, but that was not the issue. Just the fact that he thought he could walk in as he pleased had me worried.

It made me seriously wonder what went on while I was at work. That is when I found out about spy-cams but more on that in a moment. Anyway, this brings up another issue - that of letting unknown and unwelcome visitors into the house. Not only can these visitors remove anything that is lying around - they have been known to ask to use the bathroom and clean out the medicine cabinet - but other things may vanish also.

Theft is very common and drug users have sticky fingers and no regard for whose property it is. It is very difficult to be able to prove that some visitor stole from your house. Even if you know in your gut that your gold bracelet was on the coffee table where you were fixing the clasp, it would be another matter entirely to prove that the addict's friend, who just happened to stop by, actually took it.

A friend of mine allowed her boy friend to live with her for a few weeks, until she found that all her Grandmother's jewelry was missing. Again, she had no proof but by then it was too late. She never saw the jewelry again.

I had a known drug-seller come to my home looking for Jeanette. I am sure she owed him money and he came looking for it. At the time she made some flimsy excuse such as "Oh I said he could borrow my….." I never believe her for one moment, so it was one more thing to be aware of – my house was on the dealer's radar.

Obviously I was not able to be home all the time to guard my belongings, which is why I invested in the cameras. You have no way to know what security is like at your house when you are absent. Anyone may walk in and doors and windows may be left unsecured.

What about unwanted lodgers? You might come home to find unwanted people in your house. If the abuser has allowed them to come in and sleep on the floor or the sofa, it may be extremely difficult to remove them. This is one time when you will certainly have to seek legal help. Each state has its own laws regarding eviction. A lot will depend on whether the user has any legal right to the house, i.e. is his/her name on the lease or are they an owner. If so then they usually have a legal right to bring in anyone else to live there. If they are not on the lease/rental agreement and they are not an owner then you can probably get an eviction order. However, this is not always easy nor yet is it cheap. There will be legal fees and probably court costs. Meanwhile you have to deal with one or more unwanted people in your home. If they too are drug addicts, then the danger level to you and your family just hiked up another few notches.

Family Valuables

Make sure all the valuables in the house are accounted for. Are things in the right place? If you have jewelry or a coin collection, for example, is it where it is supposed to be? If a shoe box in your closet holds family valuables, are you sure that the box is not empty? Many folks have found that things have vanished - who knows when! - and the container is still sitting there giving the illusion that all is well.

An elderly friend of mine had a big coin collection which was tucked away in an unlocked cupboard. After her death it was found that the cases were all there but the coins had mysteriously vanished. Her son was known to have a big and expensive drug habit! Please do not underestimate the drug user and their ability to rationalize why it would be ok to remove stuff. They are unable or unwilling to deal with the resulting financial problems. When they are in the clutches of a drug, most common sense and family feeling has already fled.

What about other family members? Does Grandma have anything of value? If so, what I wrote above applies. Check for jewelry, guns or other weapons - Granddad's WWll service revolver will fetch quite a bit today! Sometimes it is hard to explain to an older family member that the user is really buying drugs.

If you have items that can be marked with an engraver for example, why do not so while you still have them. Alternatively, maybe a safe deposit box?

I know that you may be thinking, "Oh my son/sister/partner would never do that." Please think again. As I said above, the drug comes first ahead of any family feeling.

Financial Problems.

Financial problems almost always arise when someone in the household is a drug user. Drugs cost money. Where is that money coming from? Drugs are an expensive habit and financial problems are almost always an issue in any family where there is a user. At the same time as the user is spending money on drugs, he or she may not have as much, if any, earning power. From a doctor who is addicted to prescription medication to a son who does not work and uses street drugs, neither may be in a good financial situation. There have been many wives of prominent men who have discovered that the nest egg that they thought was safely in the bank has vanished. Likewise, an average family with a drug user may find that they have things, including cash, missing. See the section specifically on theft. Drug addicts can be very underhanded when it comes to getting their fix. Things may vanish to be sold or exchanged for drugs, and the user often has a smooth and plausible reason why the items are gone and the family is struggling with financial problems.

Andy was a successful dentist until he became an addict and alcoholic. He was in debt to the tune of more than $950,000. His wife was unaware of the extent of their financial problems and outstanding bills until they lost their lake-front house, their boat, their car and he lost his license and dental practice. His marriage finally ended when he went on the run with felony warrants in two states.

Every household is a little different but I am including a few suggestions which may be useful if you are suffering from financial problems. Maybe this will even help to avert some of them.

Money and banking.

Who is in charge of the money in the household? Do you have access to bank accounts, or are you at the financial mercy of the person who does, and who is also the user? Do you know what money comes into the household each month? These are hard things to deal with. There can be quite a bit of financial abuse if the drug abuser also controls the family money. The money will go on the drug habit long before anything like mortgage/rent is paid or food provided. Do you have any money of your own? Even a few dollars hidden away might be helpful, especially if you need to leave the house suddenly. See the section on an escape plan later in this book.

Credit Cards.

Most households have at least one credit card, and credit cards are responsible for many financial problems. Consider the following:
Do you share a credit card with the drug user?
Does the user have access to any of your cards?
Do they know your card numbers?
Can they get to your wallet or purse?
Where is your check book?

21

Are all the checks there?

If you share a credit card, do you know what the balance is?

Do you know what things are on the card?

Are there a lot of cash draws from card or bank account? Getting cash on a credit card is a very expensive way of getting money for anything but is often the way drug users get their cash.

If your name is also on the card then you are probably liable for the resulting payments. If you find out or suspect that the card is being used for drugs, you can chat with the credit card company and see if you can get you name taken off. You will probably still be liable for the bill up to the time you remove your name. You may need legal advice - but more on that in a moment.

Is the user getting money or stealing from another family member?

Are other family members having financial problems due to the drug user?

Does anyone get SNAP (food stamps) or a WIC card?

These are often stolen and traded for drugs too. It is not uncommon for a drug user to go round to each family member in turn and get money or things which can be traded or sold. Going to Grandma and telling a sad tale of needing new tires for the car, a new pair of shoes, or an outfit to help him/her get a job is not unknown.

Drug users can 'tell the tale' really well, and even if they have been found out before, they will make all kinds of rash promises to Great Aunt Mary so as to persuade her to part with some cash. I lost a generator valued at $900 and found it had been taken to a pawn shop, and they only paid out $190 for it! As it was something that was not used very often, I did not miss it immediately. Luckily, I checked around the house and realized it was gone. When questioning Jeanette I got a string of lies about its whereabouts. Fortunately I got it back, but some things never came back! I lost a lot of tools and also weird things like my bread making machine. Again, this was something I did not use that much so did not miss it until way after she was gone.

It is also not unknown for a drug user to scare another family member into providing money. It may be an older relative or a sibling. It is wise to keep an eye open for this type of abuse which is often actual blackmail or threats.

If items of value have gone it is probably a matter for the police, although I know it is hard for many families to be forced to do this.

Often you know what has gone but proving it is another matter entirely. This might be where spy cams are in order.

What if you are short of food or clothing, especially if you have children? Try a local food shelf or local Church food bank. There may not be enough money for food from the user, but food is seldom sold or exchanged for drugs, so if you find enough food for yourself and your children, you should be able to keep it. This of course, is only a stop-gap method and not one which you should continue to put up with.

It is the same with clothing - try Churches that have a clothes closet or thrift stores. Also remember that many areas have free things on Craigslist or a freecycle (Yahoo) group. Put in a request for the things you need and often people will help out.

I do not suggest any of this as a long term solution. The solution is obviously to deal with the drug use. Short term, finding a winter jacket for a child is urgent - dealing with the financial problems of a drug user will take more time.

Finally, if your partner is the income producer, but is also the drug abuser, and particularly if you have children to support, it would be smart to visit an attorney or go to Legal Aid. It is important for you to understand your legal position.

Your home whether owned or rented, is your security so please consider the following:

Is your name on the house deed or the rental agreement?

As mentioned above, are there joint credit cards and bank accounts?

What about a vehicle? Is it owned jointly?

Do you have a vehicle of your own? If so, who pays the insurance?

Is there in fact any insurance? Some people find out too late that they have no insurance (after the car is wrecked).

What about life insurance? Have any policies been cashed in? Even if you are expecting things to improve, it is much wiser get a clear picture of how you stand. Most drug abusers are not truthful, especially when it comes to money for their habit, and you will be left dealing with the financial problems of their making.

I discovered that Jeanette had taken the business check book from my purse and cleared out the account. The fact that this was our business and not her personal money-tree did not matter. She wanted drugs and that was the only thing that mattered.

The families who fare best are the ones who are proactive in dealing with the financial problems. Drug abusers are never proactive except for their drug purchases!

Theft

Let's talk a bit more about theft. Unfortunately drug users have a code which roughly states that what's theirs is theirs but what's yours is also theirs. This means that they feel free to take anything that belongs to anyone else in the home, (or anywhere else) if they can sell or trade it for drugs.

Shoplifting is very common and I discovered that Jeanette was a professional when it came to shoplifting. She and I went to a local store and I never saw her take two bottles of perfume, a pack of lighters and several small jewelry items. She denied have stolen them but I knew that she had not paid for them. I said I would go to the police but realized that it was her word against mine as I had no proof. I never went in a store with her again.

I also know that she stole from friends and acquaintances. It appeared that she would deliberately strike up an instant friendship with unsuspecting people, whine about her 'problems' for sympathy and then steal from them and leave. I saw this over and over again. I even warned one elderly woman that she was losing things that belonged to her late husband. She did not believe me so there was little I could do. Drug users manage to sound believable and can tell a good story.

There is actually a joke about meth users which says that they will steal an item from you, and then help you look for it. Sad but true.

After I had the cameras installed I saw that Jeanette rarely slept at night and often came home with bags of 'stuff'. After she left the house permanently, I found a huge stash of stolen goods. Much of this consisted of things she would never use and could not sell or trade. Shoplifting for her was a sport or a habit. I have been told that the shoplifter gets an adrenalin rush from stealing. This is similar to getting a rush from drugs but it is a pretty sad way to get your fun.

I wanted to return the items and contacted the local Sheriff, but as nothing was marked as to where it was from, the Sheriff's office could do little to return the things. They told me that their evidence room was packed with stuff like that.

Then there is the possible theft of prescription drugs belonging to other family members. There is always a street market for any kind of prescription medication. Narcotics such as Vicodin or Codeine are very popular on the street, but most other things, Ritalin for example, are also in high demand. Look out for prescription medication to be stolen or switched. If Grandma does have not good eyesight she might just be taking an aspirin in place of her prescription meds.

Check all the places where the user might have access. Remember just because the bottle is in place does not mean the contents are what the label says it is.

Identity theft and fraud is another way that users get their funds for drugs. Stealing credit cards or checks or driver's licenses, either from family members or strangers is a common way to raise money. Credit cards are either used as is, or traded to a third party for drugs.

Mail theft and fraudulently cashing Social Security payments or other forms of paper cash is also common. Bear this in mind, while keeping an eye open for mail or envelopes that are not the property of anyone in the house.

I found among Jeanette's garbage, several letters and documents, including the title of a vehicle, none of which belonged to her. Mail theft is a federal offense so this could bring the Police or Federal Agents knocking at your door. Even possession of stolen mail could cause you problems if you do not report it or attempt to return the mail.

Theft of Social Security numbers is also a money maker for drug addicts. If they have your SS number or that of your children or other family members, they can be traded for cash or drugs. There always a market for any of this stuff if the thief knows the right people.

In regards to your own mail, when you get offers for 'pre-approved-' credit cards, shred the forms immediately before dumping them in the garbage. Finally, if you have any reason to think that your mail has been stolen or tampered with, maybe it is time to get a Post Office Box for yourself. The cost is fairly moderate and the money well spent in comparison with the chaos cause by theft of your identity.

What about your computer? Do you share a computer with the addict or do they have access to yours? Is yours password protected? Just because you keep you laptop in your closet does not mean that it is safe. It can be removed and replaced while you are gone. Anyone with simple computer knowledge can open your files and probably your email. They can also check your history and see where you have been. This can be unsafe for you if, for example, you have been visiting websites on addiction or domestic violence. You might also find that anything you have viewed or written will be used by the addict for future blackmail.

One woman that I helped, found that her son had copied all the emails she had written to her sister, regarding the sister's alcoholism treatment. He threatened to pass those to the sister's employer if his mother turned him out. Addicts seem to have a way of collecting all kinds of thing against future need. See my later section for more on blackmail.

Drugs and driving

Drug users behind the wheel of a vehicle are an accident waiting to happen. On one occasion Jeanette fell asleep at the wheel of her car. Luckily, she went into a field and no one else was involved. On another occasion she mounted the pavement while trying to light a pipe while driving. Fortunately no one was standing in the way at the time or the results would have been disastrous.

All states have drunk driving laws but some do not follow laws for drugged driving. At present, there is a law known as the per se drugged driving law. This roughly states that any illegal drug found in any body fluid is considered drugged driving.

Although the media do not report so much on drugged driving, consider this; In August 2012 a woman driver in Virginia crashed her car, killing her husband and daughter. The woman had been smoking marijuana and taking prescription medications.

Another woman driver caused the death of three other women in NY State and she was found to have three prescription drugs in her system. I have no idea if these were legal prescription medications or drugs sold on the street. It makes little difference as even using marijuana can increase the risk of an accident while driving.

There is another thing to consider if the user in your home has a medical marijuana card. This does NOT protect them if they are involved in an accident while driving. Federal law does not allow marijuana for medical reasons. See the section on marijuana later in this book.

If you are concerned about the user in your household who is or may be driving while impaired, then you can check on the laws in your state. There is an excellent website at www.druggeddriving.org where you can see state-by-state information on the law of driving while under the influence of drugs.

This may be of more concern for you if the user drives your vehicle or you share insurance with them. Even more concerning is if they have other family members, especially children, as passengers. Statistics for drugged driving are pretty horrific. Drugs now appear to overtake alcohol as a leading cause of accidents. In 2009, over 6,000 people died due to drugged drivers, while 440,000 were injured. As you

can imagine, most of these injured were innocent passengers or
bystanders.

Drug use and weapons.

When ever there is a drug abuser there are almost always weapons of some kind, whether it is guns, knives, knuckle dusters, flick knives, hatchets or clubs. Aside from the fact that these can fall into the wrong hands (children for example), having any weapon in the hands of a drug addict with an attitude is not comforting.

Do you know if your drug user has weapons hidden in the home? Jeanette threatened to kill me! She owned a Colt .45 plus several other guns, and was an excellent shot. What worried me even more was the rifle with a scope on it. So if you know that there are weapons in the house be doubly careful. A mix of drugs and weapons is always unsafe.

Drug addicts do not have the balanced mental ability to safely handle a gun. Only you can assess the danger you may be in. I urge you not to make the mistake I did and think it cannot happen to you - it can!

At a minimum, if there are guns in the house they should not be loaded and should be locked in a gun safe or have a trigger lock on them. You can obtain a free gun locking kit through local law enforcement. These free kits are provided by projectchildsafe.org. Visit their website and go to the 'get a safety kit' link. You will be able to find your nearest participating law enforcement office.

If the user in your house has ever been violent then be doubly aware of anything that could be used as a weapon. For example, things that come quickly to hand, such as kitchen knives in an open rack could be discreetly put away in a drawer or cupboard.

Domestic Violence and Drug Use

Domestic violence often goes along with drug abuse so there are things you need to know to stay safe. I would like to share some information about domestic abuse to help you know and understand what it is and how to deal with it. Any time there is drug use in the home, there is a potential for violence. Understanding something about family violence, and being prepared to get away safely, will help you a lot.

The phrase domestic violence is used interchangeably with domestic abuse. Many people think that it is only domestic violence if you are physically attacked. I have heard women say, "Well he never actually hit me" This does not mean there was no abuse. So I prefer to use the term domestic abuse rather than domestic violence, as this covers all types of abuse.

Abuse comes in many forms and by the time the abuse becomes physically violent, many of the other forms of abuse are present. Abuse is about power and control and the continual diminishment of another person. It is also the slow conditioning of a person to accept the behavior of the abuser, regardless of how bizarre that behavior may be. At the present time over 90% of abusers are men, so I am going to use he/him as the abuser, although this does not mean that women cannot be abusers or that men cannot abuse other men as in a same sex relationship.

Let's break this down a bit and look more closely at the different forms of abuse: Verbal - Sexual - Economic - Physical - Emotional.

Verbal Abuse.

Some examples of Verbal Abuse would be name calling, insults, ridicule, criticism, humiliation, blame, religious and/or racial put-downs or slurs. Any of these may be done is such a way as to appear to be a joke. If the abused person does not find them funny then they are abuse and not a joke.

Unfortunately we hear a lot of verbal abuse disguised as humor in so many TV programs. All the 'dumb blond' jokes are really verbal abuse disguised as humor. The guy who says, "My wife can't think her way out of a paper bag" usually gets a laugh but at the expense of the woman. There can be further abuse if the abuser blames the victim for having no sense of humor.

Sexual Abuse.

Examples of Sexual Abuse would include rape or forced sex, (it does not matter whether you are married to the person or not, forced sex is sexual abuse). Unnatural or unwanted sexual acts, unwelcome touching/fondling of a sexual nature, sadistic sex, or being forced to look at sexual material (magazines or videos) or watch/hear sexual activity. Also being threatened with such things as "If you don't agree or let me do this, I will have to....find a prostitute...use your daughter.....throw you and the kids out" This is blackmail but more on that in a moment.

Economic Abuse.

Economic Abuse is almost always present in a home where one person is a drug user. Any income goes first for the drugs and only then do other things get paid. Rent or food or utilities often get ignored. Economic abuse also includes the drug user controlling all the income. Even if the partner works, her paycheck is turned over to the user/abuser. Needs can be withheld. For example, the need for medical care, glasses or dental care, or the partner can be trapped, for example, by having no shoes in the winter so she cannot leave the house.

Emotional Abuse.

Emotional abuse is not the same as direct verbal abuse but it is just as damaging although more subtle. Emotional abuse can include subversive manipulation, mind games, controlling by guilt trips, depriving a person of sleep which is often couched as "I need to talk to you" or "I want sex and more sex". Passive-aggressive behavior is also emotional abuse. A good example of passive aggressive behavior is the partner who 'forgets' important things; an anniversary, a meeting, paying a bill or bringing home diapers from the store. Often times they will make a joke of it when confronted. Part of this can be due to the drugs being used and part can also be quite intentional passive-aggressive behavior.

Emotional abuse is present in all the different forms of abuse I have previously listed, but is also a powerful form of abuse on its own. The abuser appears to be supportive but undermines the victim in many subtle ways and always sounds very reasonable about it. May try to 'fix' the victim, and often lets everyone know he is doing it for her own good.

Physical Abuse.

Finally there is Physical Abuse which really needs little explanation. Hitting, slapping, punching, kicking, biting, choking, or any kind of forcible restraint is, obviously, physical abuse. Along with that there are threatening actions which are physical but not enough to cause serious injury. For example, blocking - standing in the way so that you have to request that the other person moves (giving him/her power) or having to push him/her away (giving an excuse for more physical violence).

Jeanette flew into a huge rage with me on one occasion while I was holding an unloaded air rifle. She grabbed my shirt and pulled me down, and the end of the rifle cut her cheek so badly she needed stitches. She later told a judge in court that I had attacked her and cut her face deliberately. This is how things get twisted so that nothing is ever their fault. There were many instances where it was just my word against hers.

What does abuse feel like to the victim?

Almost all abusers follow a cycle which is so well known that it is called the Cycle of Abuse. The Cycle of Abuse has three fairly predictable stages, and looks something like this:

The **Tension Building Stage**; Threats may be made, small incidents of violence used, and the abuser may have a particular way of letting the victim know that he is building up to an acute abuse episode. It may be remarks, it could be sarcasm or he could be distant. Eventually the victim will recognize this stage as a pre-requisite for the actual acute abuse. Drug use may escalate or the lack of drugs or the ability to pay for drugs may cause the abuser to build towards the acute abuse.

At some point the phase of **Acute Abuse** occurs, either severe battering or explosions of temper or sexual activity. This can also be a drug binge or the user being gone for days at a time with no contact. These are often timed to catch the victim off-guard, such as when visitors are expected, or when they were preparing to go out to dinner.

If the woman threatens to leave/call the police etc, the abuser will do everything in his power to stop her. This is often known as the **Honeymoon Stage** where he uses loving, contrite behavior. He will be apologetic and appear caring and considerate. He may make assurances of his love or cry or beg on his knees and promise it will never happen again. The drug user will promise to stop using and go to a rehab.

Once the victim allows him to dissuade her from action, his cycle of violence is complete. This phase may last from a few days to a few weeks but slowly the cycle begins all over again. Naturally, the user has no intention of stopping his drug use or going into rehab.

Once the victim accepts the assurance, this same pattern will be followed time and time again. When a drug user finds something that works, they continue to make it work to their advantage.

An abuser almost always places the blame for the abuse on the woman or some outside circumstance.

"She made me mad",

"If she hadn't done..... I would not have had to hit her",

"She knows not to bug me when I've been drinking",

"I was out of dope".

There is never ever any justification for abuse. This type of excuse is an admission of the lack of personal power and also a lack of willingness to be responsible for one's own actions. By admitting that some external force can 'make you' hit someone, shows that there is no control over self. These people are giving their personal power away to a set of circumstances.

If you have not already thought about making an escape plan, see my suggestions for making one. Even if you think you do not need one, please make one anyway. When you are dealing with a drug user, you can never really know if they will turn violent. Drug use along with any tendency to violence makes for an unsafe situation.

Even if you are not expecting violence, if there are guns or other weapons in the home, consider these safety issues, or look at my personal list of safety ideas later in this book. If you already know that the drug user in your family is violent, please take some action NOW. Do not wait until you are badly hurt or dead. More women are killed by an abusive partner than are killed by a stranger.

All abuse, of whatever kind, is a need for power and control. Many abusers get a 'high' from the abuse, in the same way that the addict gets a 'high' from a hit of dope. No one keeps good records on a national level of the number of women who are abused each year but it has been suggested that there are in excess of four million. Please, do not become one of them. There are ways to get free. There are steps you can take to keep yourself, your children and even your pets safe.

Once I had the cameras installed and set up I also saw that my old and almost-blind dog was kicked by Jeanette. It was a good thing that by the time I saw what she had done, she was already gone from the house. Otherwise I might just have resorted to some abuse of my own!

If you are attacked and you call the police, depending on the laws of your state, it is most likely that the abuser will get arrested. You might need to check on the laws though, as in some states, both parties could be arrested. This is especially true if the abuser tries to blame you for the attack.

If the abuser is arrested, he may only be booked and then released. He may be given a conditional release which means that he cannot come back to the residence or in any other way interfere with you. This is on paper but in fact does not necessarily protect you from an abusers actions. The abuser will no doubt blame you for his arrest and possibly seek immediate vengeance.

If he is arrested you can find out from the local jail if he is being released. You can ask that you be informed of his release but sometimes you do not get much notice and sometimes none. Laws vary from state to state on this. Do be pushy about asking though, as this could save your life.

Jeanette was released at 3:00am after attacking me and even though she had a conditional release prohibiting her from coming near me, she was back at the house by 4:30am. By the time this happened I was much more aware of what she was capable of and was ready for her to return. I also had the cameras in place to document the fact that she returned.

This kind of situation is when you use your escape planning and go to a friend, family member, motel or shelter. You are also entitled to file for a restraining order. Again this is not a guarantee of your safety so as well as a court order you will have to be pro-active in keeping yourself safe. The mistake that many people make is that they do not consider seriously enough that they could be the target of violence and that they could be seriously hurt or killed. I made the same mistake. I never thought that Jeanette would attack me like she did. I was lucky - I got away from her. Had she been holding a gun or a knife I may not have been so lucky.

Lying

I have listed lying separately as I have never known of a drug user who does not also lie. They lie continuously about everything from the large important things down to the smallest and most inconsequential things.

Dealing with a liar is exhausting at best and combine this with drug use makes for a situation that is hell to live with. They will lie about their drug use, they will lie about the whereabouts of money, they will lie about missing items and if you confront them about these lies, they will lie more to cover what they have done.

To be a good liar, you really need a good memory. This is one thing where a drug user will give the game away as their memory is not good, so they will never remember what lie they previously told you. It is painful to know that a member of your family and someone you love is a habitual liar. Sometimes it is harder to accept that than the drug use.

One woman who contacted me said she was aware that her son was using cocaine but it was when she realized that he was lying and continuing to lie to her about many things that it hurt the most. I dealt with lies and then more lies to cover previous lies. I think that her continuous lying was one of the main things that were so difficult to live with. It was sad to know that I could not trust one single thing that came out of her mouth.

Whenever I confronted Jeanette about something where she lied, she turned it round and told me that it was my fault, that I had not understood her correctly. If all else failed she resorted to a temper tantrum and slammed out of the house. Never once did she admit to lying.

There are a few things to remember when dealing with a liar.

It is not your fault.

No, they do NOT lie to protect you.

You are not too stupid to understand the truth.

It will be difficult if not impossible to trust them again.

If you do decide to trust, then trust but verify.

Finally, if they are still using drugs then they will still be lying.

You may also have another problem to deal with. You might find, as I did, that lies are spread far and wide about you. As no one actually comes out and tells you what is being said, this is hard to counter. I found out through anonymous letters many things that I was supposed to have done, none of which were true. It made living in a small town very uncomfortable. I finally wrote an open letter to the local newspaper, just saying that any and all anonymous letters would be forwarded to the police. That effectively stopped the letters but I am sure it did nothing to stop the lies.

Blackmail.

Both abusers and drug users often use some forms of blackmail to get what they want. The blackmail may be threats of things that they can or might do. For example, "I'll tell Child Protective Services that you have a problem and they will take your kids away" or possibly "Give me some money or I will come down to your workplace and get it from you there". There is also the emotional type of blackmail such as the things Jeanette tried, "I really need money for gas to get to work or I lose my job". When asked where her last paycheck went, there was always another excuse "I had to buy a new tire… I had to get my glasses fixed…..I needed some new shoes" The list went on and on.

She tried this tactic with her Mother and it usually worked although the money was never repaid. After her mother died, I got the calls at my place of work, where she threatened me if I did not lend/give her money. The threats escalated into screaming matches, including threats of suicide, and I am surprised that the neighbors never called the police. She had been known to walk up and down the street where I worked, screaming abuse into her cell phone.

Many families have things that they would prefer not to have shouted to the world. As I mentioned earlier, drug addicts like to hang on to any bits of information, either real or imagined, in the hope they can benefit from the blackmail in times of need. As hard as it is, it is better not to allow the drug user to dictate what you do with blackmail threats. The blackmail will only continue or get worse. When they do not get what they want, they will try and up the ante.

I knew that Jeanette might get arrested in the street. She might also have got arrested while buying drugs or shoplifting. I knew there was nothing I could do about that and I would have to deal with whatever happened.

There is also the issue of enabling when people are threatened by the user. I had one mother tell me it was easier to do what her son wanted than have him cause problems at her work. Although I understand that she did not want to lose her job, she was also enabling him to continue to hold this threat over her. He finally became violent and broke her arm. She would certainly have been in less pain had she dealt with his blackmail threats sooner. I have more information on enabling under triggering a drug user.

Drug dealing

Drug dealing kicks up the danger factor yet another notch. Drug dealing is very bad news. Jeanette was allowing drug deals on my front porch. I only found out by installing hidden spy cameras. When I saw what was happening at my house in my absence I was appalled. I realized that a number of people knew my address and what my house looked liked and these were people who were the local drug users, were dangerous and who were known to the police/sheriff.

The penalties for drug dealing can be severe. Children in the home can be initially put into care for their own safety. The police or sheriff may come with a warrant and search your home. A home invasion is another threat that comes with dealing drugs. Your house or car may be broken in to or damaged. It is not unknown for a buyer who feels cheated to do a payback with paint stripper on your vehicle or worse.

Drug wars are common. If the person selling drugs infringes on the 'turf' of another seller, gang violence can escalate quickly. Many drive-by shootings are due to these kinds of turf wars. Once it is known that your house contains drugs, you are high on the list for some very unwelcome visitors.

If you have any idea that the user in your household is dealing drugs, then you need to treat this as an emergency situation and think about getting yourself and any children and your animals to a place of safety.

Marijuana; grown for use or profit.

Currently (2012) there are about 17 states where it is legal to use medical marijuana but four of these states do not allow you to grow your own and two more states have special requirements. I found a fairly good list of states allowing growing etc at http://www.procon.org/ and they appear to update their information to reflect newer laws.

All states who allow growing currently have a limit on the number of plants that are allowed, varying from about six to sixteen. This is not the place for me to discuss the pros and cons of using marijuana, as I want to focus on the possible dangers of any marijuana grow, regardless of whether it is legal or not. In my home state of Oregon it is legal to grow your own if you have a medical marijuana card. However, there are still safety issues to consider.

One family had their legal grow stolen by a teenage boy who promptly sold the weed at the local high school. Another family with an illegal grow also had their crop stolen, this time by another family member. So regardless of whether the grow is legal or not, you will still face the possibility of a break-in and theft.

There is also another and bigger issue. Federal law does not allow the growing of marijuana. DEA officials can and do raid growers, even in states where the grows are allowed by state law. Federal law overrides state law. DEA officials can take the whole crop and all the growing equipment if they so choose. So, just because your state says it is OK, you may still be in trouble with the DEA. The bottom line here is that just because it is legal in your state does not mean that the state can or will protect you from seizure. If word gets around that you are growing marijuana, even legally, you may get some unwelcome visitors.

Methamphetamine production

Meth production is serious trouble. Acquaintances of mine, a couple in their mid 50's, had no idea that their 22 year old son was running a meth lab in their barn. Not, that is, until the place went up in a fireball while they were out of town. The barn was a total loss and the son was severely burned. Even now, years later, he cannot walk properly and has lost the sight in one eye. Producing meth is like sitting with an unexploded bomb.

Now you may think that you would know if the user in your home was cooking meth. Well, maybe not. A small meth cooking unit can be set up and taken down easily. Cooks have been known to use motel rooms, cars, trailers and tents as well as any shed, barn or storage space. The biggest tip-off might be the odor. Meth is made from very nasty smelly stuff including lye, paint thinner, sulfuric or muriatic acid, red phosphorus and acetone to name just a few. Another tip-off would be stained Pyrex cookware or coffee filters. In fact any strong chemical odors or unexplained stains could spell trouble.

If you think your user has been cooking meth, do not touch anything in the area. This is a matter for the police and a professional (Hazmat) clean up crew. These chemical mixes are very toxic and also flammable. Get away from any suspect area immediately. Meth can also cling to any place where it is made so walls, curtains, carpets or clothing can hang on to the chemicals. For this reason, even if the user is not cooking meth in or near your home, but is cooking somewhere else, they can still bring toxins into the house when they return. Even the smoking of crystal meth can contaminate clothing which is then toxic, especially to children.

Any contact with meth and the chemicals used during manufacture will result in health problems. These could include headache, nausea, fatigue, chest pain and difficulty breathing. Children may be especially susceptible. If you are noticing any unexplained health issues, toxins from meth manufacture could be the cause.

There is yet another way now for meth to be made which is in some ways is even more dangerous. This is known as the bottle method or the shake-and-bake method. This is where a small quantity of meth is made in something like a 2 liter soda bottle. Users get the recipe from the Internet or from friends and then try making it for themselves. The biggest danger is that this can easily go wrong and explode into a huge fireball.

Even if the bottle does not explode, the residue in the bottle is toxic and corrosive. If you find any soda bottle that looks at all suspicious, do not open it! In fact do not touch it at all. If it contains meth residue it can easily explode. This is also time for the police and the Hazmat team, who are trained to deal with these things. This is so vital that I am going to say this again. Do not touch any suspect soda bottle even if it was dumped in your yard by a passer by. These chemicals are volatile and very dangerous.

There are other newer 'designer' drugs on the streets now, including Bath Salts that are equally as dangerous as meth. Many of these new drugs can send the user into a frenzy of hyper-activity. These reactions can begin fast and affect a user who is normally non-aggressive.

Even as Bath Salts are being banned, other drugs similar in nature are being produced in an effort to dodge the law. The end user has no idea what is in these chemical concoctions and there is no way to know how any person will be affected. Symptoms of Bath Salts or use of a similar drug is often extremely high body temperature where clothing may be ripped off, paranoia, delusions and hallucinations. If the user in your home suddenly displays any of these signs it is time to grab your emergency bag and leave.

Triggers: What might trigger a drug user?

Some times it is impossible to tell what might trigger a crisis, but there are other, fairly universal things, that are calculated to cause the drug user to flip out. Lack of drugs or the ability to find or pay for drugs makes users paranoid and angry. Drug withdrawal is uncomfortable at best and life threatening at its worst. Any drug user will do anything and everything to avoid withdrawal. For example, if a user has been in the habit of obtaining drugs in a fairly regular way from one source, and then that source suddenly vanishes, the user will be panicked. They may steal from your purse/wallet or take something of value and if you get in the way you could get hurt.

Enabling.

Withdrawing your support is another thing that could trigger trouble. If you have been in the habit of enabling in any way, then stopping the enabling is likely to cause them to up the ante. I mentioned enabling earlier, but do you understand about enabling? When there is an addict in a family setting there is almost certain to be some enabling that allows the addict to continue their way of life. Painful as it is, we have to face it. The other family members may adjust their lifestyle or lie to cover for the addict.

For example:

"My husband is too sick to come to work today."

"I have to take care of my daughter's children or they would not eat."

"My son stays in bed all day while I work and then goes out all night."

"My brother is always borrowing money from our Mother and she keeps giving it to him even though she is on a pension."

"If I didn't let my daughter live here she would be living on the street."

I have heard stories like this from many people. What these people are doing is allowing the addict to continue their downhill spiral into drugs. I do understand how painful it is to see your child, or partner, in the grip of drugs. Most parents or spouses for that matter want to 'protect' their children or partner long after they should be caring for themselves. Some times this is due to the shame of not wanting anyone to know what is happening in the family. This may be especially true of the family if they are well respected in the community; a doctor, a lawyer, a business person or even a pastor. No family is above having a drug using member.

Parents may be contributing to the drug use at the expense of their own health, comfort, safety and well being. Mothers especially are often in a caregiver role, working to support adult children who do not work or contribute anything. Partners often do the same thing especially if there are children involved and the drug user is also the income producer.

If your user is also bringing in income, however small or erratic, you most likely take care not to upset him/her for fear of even more trauma or abuse. Many partners or parents also minimize the drug use and the problems it causes.

If you want the drug user in your family to stop using drugs, you need to look at your own supporting role. The drug user often continues their use by using fear tactics. Men may use violence or the threat of violence against their partners or their children. Women can do similar things and sometimes with a twist, such as self-mutilation and then threatening to call the police to say it was the partner who caused the injury.

A great many household things may be destroyed or just vanish. I lost a lot of tools and the generator before I put a stop to the enabling. Yes, I did my share of enabling until I came to realize that it was actually helping her to use drugs. I was part of the problem! I paid bills, gave her money for 'shoes' or 'car repairs' and in many other ways contributed to her drug use.

I actually did more and more while she got away with doing less and less. It was easier for me to do it myself than listen to her moan or complain or throw china or a temper tantrum. So, I understand first hand what it feels like, but, YOU MUST STOP YOUR PART IN THE ENABLING PROCESS. For as long as you continue to let the drug user continue to use at your expense, they will not stop and the use will most likely increase.

Changing the Pattern.

You will have to lay down firm ground rules and stick to them. For example, when dealing with teens, the removal of privileges such as cell phone, computer etc could be a start. Talking with their school should also be included.

For an adult child, a deadline for them to get a place of their own and a job. These things should go along with some kind of drug abuse therapy. For a partner, a family intervention, possibly drug rehab and counseling as well. Bottom line is; if you go on doing what you are doing, you will go on getting what you are getting. The drug user will not change the balance if it is to their advantage so YOU MUST.

Sadly, there is another thing to think about. The user may not want to stop. Even though you see the damage that the drug use does to the family, the user may not see or want to see or be able to stop. Getting away from drugs involves hard work. It involves looking at previous behavior. It means taking responsibility for actions. Some users are not able to do that. This does not mean that you, the family, should go on supporting them.

Let me put it this way. You will most likely lose the user in some way, unless and until they decide for themselves, to stop using. You can choose to stop the enabling behavior and accept that the user may move away from you, or that you will be forced to leave the user. Or you can continue to allow their behavior and watch them deteriorate and possibly die from drug use. In the meantime, the damage that they are inflicting on the whole family is totally toxic.

Now there are risks in stopping the enabling because the user will not like it. This is where you have to judge the risk factor and plan accordingly. If the drug user has ever been violent, then you need to seriously plan how you are going to be safe.

I gradually withdrew the enabling that I had been doing with Jeanette. She knew I was aware of her drug use and she became very angry. I slowly cut off ways for her to get money for drugs. I removed all valuables belonging to me. I put a lock on my bedroom door. Every time I changed something, she threw a temper tantrum. I did have to deal with a lot of verbal abuse and screaming while planning to get away from her. I made sure I remained calm and did not confront her, thus giving her any chance to become violent with me.

When she used her screaming or guilting tactics, I merely said in a calm voice, "I am sorry you are upset but I don't know what to tell you". It made her very mad and she did her best to make me respond and get angry, but I refused to be drawn in to a fruitless argument. She was totally irrational by this time and I knew the smallest thing could set her off.

She was also a self-mutilator, often cutting herself or hitting her head on the wall. She also threatened suicide on a number of occasions. When she did finally attack me, it was after days of being awake on meth and she was at the tweaking stage. I was actually leaving the house and had my back to her, going out the front door when she jumped at me, knocking me down. There was no confrontation between us, so to this day I do not know why she did what she did. This is why I say that you can never be sure that the user will not become violent.

Making an Escape Plan

Even if you do not think you are in an unsafe situation, please make an escape plan. Better to have a plan and never use it, than to need to leave and find you cannot. Please understand that these suggestions are meant to cover your safety for now. This is not a way you should live permanently. The drug or abuse issues must be addressed and dealt with.

So, this is a stop gap method for the short term, to keep you safe. If you are threatened, do not hesitate to call 911. This is especially important if you have children.

Please consider some of the following and see what things apply to your situation.

Do you have money? What I mean by that is; do you have access to some emergency money, should you need to call a cab, rent a motel room, use a public phone or get a train or bus. Even $20 stashed away will be something but more if you can manage it. Leave it with a family member or a trusted friend (more on that in a minute), hide it outside the home somewhere, get a savings account or stash it in your emergency bag. (see below).

Is there someone you can trust? If you are in need of making an escape plan, then you will also need as much support as possible. Do you have a family member close by or a friend who you can trust? If so, good! However, they have to live close enough for you to get to them with little or no money, and possibly in the middle of the night.

If possible have a second place for some emergency cash. A drug crazed abuser may take your purse, car keys, wallet, and anything else that may help you get away. Your cell phone may also vanish and for that reason you might want to consider getting a cheap 'disposable' phone if you can afford it. The price for these phones has dropped a lot over the past few years and the small expenditure is worth it in the safety it provides.

Whatever you do, do not get into a confrontation with a tweaker or someone who is violent. Also remember that the abuser may threaten your friends or family. For that reason it might be safer for you to find out where your local Women's Shelter is located. They are used to dealing with violent partners. Often they will pick up a woman from a well-lighted place such as a convenience store or gas station. Get their number and make a note of it in your bag.

Get a spare car key. If you need to leave, it will have to be done in such a way that you do not arouse the suspicions of the user. Hide a spare car key if possible. Then if your keys vanish you will be able to get to the spare.

Create an emergency bag. This is vital. Get copies of any important papers such as birth certificates, for you and any children, any identity cards, credit card numbers, driving license number and anything else such as numbers from insurance policies, and copies of medical records. Don't forget medication and include a few days supply which can be rotated every few weeks. Keep your bag up to date. If you have room, throw in a few spare clothes, some energy bars or other high energy snacks and possibly a bottle or two of water.

Include a flashlight and a small first aid kit. A toothbrush, spare glasses or your glasses prescription, and personal hygiene items plus some wet wipes. If you have children to pack for too, think about a few diapers, a change of clothing and a few small toys or books.

If you have children old enough to be able to carry a small backpack, then pack things for them to carry. Many of these things can be found at your local dollar store. Don't worry if you cannot get everything immediately, just do the best you can. Building up your bag bit by bit can be a great confidence boost.

Chose a safe location for the bag, preferably with a close friend, neighbor or family member. However, remember that a drug user who is also an abuser will probably know where you are likely to go. Be careful.

Depending on where you live, also think about how you might be able to safely exit the house. Consider children and pets too. Know a number of ways to leave plus ways out of your neighborhood. Abusers have been known to try and run down a fleeing spouse with a vehicle.

While on the subject of pets, if you have a beloved pet and want to be able to take Fluffy or Fido with you, then make some provision for them too. Find a carrier for a cat or small animal with a towel or small sheet to cover it and a small dish for water inside.

A leash for Fido and a few dog treats and remember a couple of small plastic bags for garbage or poopy pickup. If you have a friend or neighbor who will take in your pet, so much the better. Ask ahead of time. It is not unknown for abusers to injure or kill a pet in a rage.

Please take some action now and make a plan. If you are helping someone else, encourage them to make an escape plan, but do not get between an addict and his victim. Call the police!

What to tell your children.

Dealing with children in a home where there is a drug addict is not at all easy. On the one hand, you do not want to alarm them unnecessarily but on the other hand, they may already know there are problems. Often children fear what they cannot understand so I believe it is best to be as truthful as possible with children. Obviously you will have to tailor what you say to the child's age and ability to understand.

One idea might be to talk about being ready for any kind of emergency. There is a good government site with helpful tips for parents at http://www.ready.gov/kids. Even though this is intended for natural disasters, there is some good information and ways to make getting an emergency kit together a fun activity. By helping your children to put together an emergency disaster kit, you are preparing them for dealing with adult issues in a pretty non-threatening way. Then, if you need to leave you home fast due to the drug user, the children will already be aware of grabbing their kit, (packed in a small backpack) and not be so afraid.

The older the child, the more they will be able to understand about drug use. You can explain that there is a difference between loving someone and not liking what they do. Therefore, you can say that we love Daddy (or brother or sister or whoever) but we do not like what they are choosing do. It is not necessarily the person who is bad, but the choices they are making are not healthy ones. This can be a very valuable learning experience for children, scary though it may seem.

If there is or has been violence in the house then you need to prepare your children a little more. For example, do they know how to use a phone? Depending on their age, can they get to and use a cell phone? Can they say their full name and their address? Do they know what to do if you are attacked? Do they understand about calling 911? Arrange a safe and secure place for them to go to, either a neighbor or local store or possibly a safe place to hide. Make a plan with them ahead of time and make sure they know what they should do.

Have you set up a secret safety code with your children? This is a good idea for any family. It works like this. You come up with a short easy to remember word or phrase which they will ONLY use if they are in danger. So if you speak to them on the phone and they say their secret code to you, then you know that there is something wrong. This works if you are at work and speak to them at home or if they are at a friend's house or the Mall. Make it clear that this is a secret safety code and no one else should know what it is. Also it should only be used for serious safety situations.

You can also set up a similar thing for you to say to them, if, for example you want them to leave the house fast in a situation where you might be attacked. This would be a signal for them to run to their safe place and call 911.

There is some very good general safety information for parents at http://www.fcgov.com/police/pdf/childsafe.pdf. You can download it from that site and use it to prepare your children to be safe.

Restraining Orders and Stalking Orders

Do you understand the difference between Restraining Orders and Stalking Orders? The information provided here is to give you an overview of restraining orders and stalking orders. **I am not an attorney and this is not legal advice.** Laws vary from state to state and I urge you to become familiar with the laws in your state.

Restraining Orders.

These are sometimes called protective orders. They are legal documents issued by a judge to keep an abuser away from his victim. It may also give you temporary custody of any children, make the abuser move from the home, require that the abuser stay away not only from the home but also your place of work, school or any other place you may be.

You can ask for a restraining order against your spouse or an ex-spouse, anyone in your family or a domestic partner of either sex, if they have been abusive towards you.

To obtain an order you will need to contact your local court. If you do not know where to find them, your local police or sheriff or women's shelter will be able to direct you. There will be papers you need to fill out. Be sure to be completely truthful when filling out the paperwork, but do not be afraid to say why you are scared of the abuser. If the abuser threatened to harm you or your children, you need to put that down so that the judge knows what has happened. It can be embarrassing to have to tell about some things, but remember these people are there to help and protect you. If you do not tell them everything, they will not be able to do a good job. This is not a time to be shy.

After the paperwork is filled out you will have to get it signed by a judge. The clerk of the court will be able to explain more about the procedure in your area. You can also ask if they have a victim assistance office or an abused women's advocate. Often there will be someone there to help you with the forms and even go into the courtroom with you. You will probably be called in front of a judge who may ask you questions. Try not to be embarrassed but answer the judge's questions and explain why you want this order.

After the order is signed, it will have to be served on the abuser. Often the local Sheriff can do that, but again, ask what the procedure is. The order is not in effect until the abuser had been served with a copy.

Remember that this order can only go so far in keeping you safe. Abusers can ignore a court order especially if they are using drugs or alcohol to cloud their thinking. They may have so much rage that they do not care if they get caught so long as they get even or can hurt you. You have to do your part to stay safe.

I have some suggestions which I used to protect myself. If your abuser breaks the order and comes to your home or work, even if he does not harm or threaten you, you need to call the police. If you allow him to flout the order, for example if he says he is just picking up his clothes, it will be harder in future to make the court understand that you are serious. By the way, in the case of an abuser living with you who needs clothes, work tools or the like, you can have the police or a sheriff do a 'stand by' which gives the abuser 20 minutes or so to get his belongings.

Once you have a restraining order in place, the other party has a chance to oppose the order. You may have to attend court to tell your side of the story. Be sure to keep all court dates or speak with the court clerk if for some reason you cannot be there. Restraining orders can be granted for a short time, i.e. if there are children involved, and then a court hearing will decide on visitation etc. Then a more permanent order can be put into place which will need to be renewed, most likely after a year.

Stalking Orders.

The requirements for a stalking order are different from those of a restraining order. You can obtain a stalking order against anyone who is stalking you, not necessarily a family member or even someone that you know. The criteria for a stalking order are that there is "*intentional harassment of another person that places the other person in reasonable fear for that person's safety.*" There must also be "*two or more separate acts over a period of time, showing a "continuity of purpose" that would cause a reasonable person to suffer substantial emotional distress.*"

I filed for and got a stalking order against Jeanette with the help of the cameras at my house, which caught her continually driving by and bothering someone staying in the house. Stalking orders can be obtained against an abuser if the restraining order is not stopping the abuser from following you, waiting outside your workplace or school or telephoning you.

Jeanette also started phoning me at all hours of the night but hanging up when I answered the phone or leaving messages which consisted entirely of cuss words. I replayed these onto a small tape and handed them to the DA at the court.

In short, a restraining order mostly protects against actual contact, while a stalking order prevents the abuser from following you or harassing you in any way. This also applies to a third party trying to contact you on the abusers behalf. If you have an order in place and a friend tries to speak to you, telling you that it is OK for you to talk to them, HANG UP! They tried this with me but I knew the law and just hung up. The only communication that can be made is through the court, the DA or the attorney involved.

The very best advice I can give you is to find out about these things in advance. Even if you do not think you will ever need this help, a few phone calls will give you some information so you will know what to do should things get really bad.

Suicide or Overdose

Suicide is a subject that few people want to consider. However, if you have a drug addict in the family you need to give this at the very least, some consideration. Drug use raises the risk of suicide or sudden death for both men and women, but women are for some reason at greater risk for suicide. If an unsuccessful suicide attempt has been made by the user, then subsequent attempts are a real possibility. Depression or mental illness increases this risk also.

If the user has already displayed violent tendencies, then the risk rises even further. According to information on the Government website of SAMHSA (Substance Abuse and Mental Health Services) use of drugs and alcohol increase the chance of suicide by at least 6%. In 2011 over 30,000 Americans committed suicide, and half of all suicides were men between the ages of 25 and 65. For youngsters ages 15 to 25 it is now the third leading cause of death. Over 70% of these suicides involved drug or alcohol use.

You can see from these statistics that suicide is a real possibility with a drug user. There is another aspect of this and that is death by accidental overdose. In particular, death by overdosing on pain medications is at an all time high. Over 36,000 deaths from overdose were reported as far back as 2008. Both prescription medications, regardless of whether obtained from street sales or legally, and heroin use can result in overdose due to these drugs depressing breathing. They also make it harder for people to remember if/when they used or took a dose.

A lot of concern has surfaced in the past few years regarding the use or overuse of antidepressants, especially for young people. It appears that many of the shooters in recent crime spree killings were on some type of antidepressant. When we also know that many prescription drugs are diverted from the original patient and sold on the streets, it is even more concerning. People mistakenly believe that if it is a prescription drug then it is safe to take. The problem here is that even with assessments from a health professional, serious side effects from these drugs are fairly common. In the case of someone buying off the street or from a friend or neighbor, the user is totally unsupervised. Even their close family may not know what they are taking.

Many antidepressants now carry a warning mandated by the FDA regarding possible symptoms.

Anxiety, agitation, panic attacks, insomnia, irritability, hostility aggressiveness, impulsivity, akathisia (psychomotor restlessness), hypomania, and mania, have been reported in adult and pediatric patients being treated with antidepressants for major depressive disorder as well as for other indications, both psychiatric and nonpsychiatric.

However these warnings are unlikely to follow the sale of these medications on the streets. Even if they are seen they are likely to be ignored or dismissed.

What does this mean for you? Knowing what drugs are being used by the addict is important. Overdosing on marijuana is not as likely as overdosing on vicodin or heroin. Understand what other things might trigger an actual suicide attempt too, mental illness for example.

You might also want to consider what happens if the drug addict dies. Is this person the income producer? If so, how will you manage? Is there any life insurance? Does the insurance cover suicide? These are hard things to consider, but better to think about them now than wait until the almost unthinkable happens and then have to deal with it.

Because Jeanette was a self-abuser I knew she had the capability for violence. She threatened suicide several times, partly as a blackmail ploy to get money from me. I told her I was going to call the Sheriff and I did. I had to take the risk that she would not seriously harm herself, but at the same time, I knew that there was nothing that I could do that would alter what she intended. I was not willing to let her continue to use the threat of suicide as blackmail.

Safety Ideas from my personal experience.

I have added these safety ideas in the hope that they may be helpful for you to keep yourself and your family safe and secure. No matter whether you continue in the same house that you shared with the user or you have moved to another address, you need to be aware of your continuing safety.

After Jeanette attacked me I had to make a number of changes in my life and in my household. After I obtained the stalking order, I still knew I was the person most responsible for my own safety.

Cell Phone:

My cell phone is with me day and night. I make sure it is fully charged and I have the local sheriff's number programmed into it. I know that many people today carry a cell phone and it is one of the best safety ideas that I know, but I also know that there is the expense issue. However, most cell phones, even if they are not activated with a cell company, will still call 911.

Even if you have an older phone, or if you cannot afford to activate a phone, still carry it with you. You should be able to check with the original carrier about its ability to call in an emergency. Also many women's shelters provide phones for women to use in an emergency, so if you do not have access to a phone it would be worth asking at your local shelter.

What if your abuser knows your cell or house number and calls you as Jeanette did to me? Try using a disposable phone for a while and turning your other phones off. That way you can leave it on at night but you will be sure no one will call and harass you at 2:00am.

Phone Number:

I changed my home phone number to an unlisted one and am very careful to whom I give it. I have caller ID so can usually tell who is on the line before I answer. If I do not recognize the number I allow the call to roll over to the message.

Locks:

I changed all the locks on all the doors. I installed deadbolts on all outside doors and safety bars on sliding doors. I also installed window locks on the windows of the rooms I used, and actually screwed some windows shut in areas that I was not using. Be aware though that this is not a good idea if you might need these windows as a safety exit, in case of a fire for example. Never do this on a bedroom window.

Even if you barely know a screwdriver from a hammer you can probably figure out how to do a lot of this for yourself. Changing locks is pretty easy. Take a look at the locks you currently have. Even take a picture if you can and armed with this, go to your local hardware store. Explain that you need to change just the lock and ask for their help. They will be able to show you what will be a good replacement. Some locks just require the barrel be switched which is easy. For others they may suggest an upgrade to a tougher lock.

Deadbolts are the best protection as the older handle type locks are pretty easy to open. There are also surface deadbolts which may be a little easier to install.

Many homes have an additional chain device on their front door. These are designed to allow you to open the door enough to see who is there. These chains are, for the most part, pretty useless. They are not very strong and can easily be broken with a determined shove on the door. Look for a better quality bar-type security device if you need to see who is at the door. It is really safer to use a spy-hole in the door or a camera before opening the door to anyone.

If you do not feel able to drill a hole for a deadbolt, ask at the place where you get your locks if they know of any handyman service which is not too expensive. I have found that when you explain the situation, many people are willing to help you out. One of the guys at my local hardware store does small customer jobs on the side, so there is a good chance that if you ask, they will know someone who will help you. Alternatively get a good locksmith as he will be able to determine the best way for you to say safe.

If you are in a rented home, ask the landlord or the rental company to change the locks and explain why you need it done fast. If you feel unsafe, go to another location or find someone to stay with you for a few days.

Another good idea is to get a door security bar such as those that you can take with you to a motel. They do not attach to the door but do prevent entry. They are available at places like Lowes, Target etc and are fairly inexpensive. You can also find door alarms that are battery operated. When disturbed they emit ear piercing shrieks!

You can also purchase a couple of good big bolts for the top and bottom of the outside doors. Again, these are pretty easy to fix yourself and do provide fairly good protection against an intruder when you are home. If you have doors with glass panels, these can be easily broken and a hand can be passed through and the door unlocked.

It is the same with small windows next to the door. Bolts normally cannot be reached from a small window in the door. If you have floor to ceiling windows close to the door, this is more of a problem, and a keyed deadbolt is probably the best option. Just be sure you have the key where you can get it easily at night in case of the need for a fast exit, a fire for example.

You might also want to consider getting the glass replaced with Plexiglas, which will not break or shatter like glass. If your outer door is all glass (some back entrances are like this) think about getting a metal safety screen door. Even though many are not that tough, it does provide another layer of security between you and any intruder.

While on the subject of fire, do you have a working fire extinguisher? It is always a good idea to have at least one in the house, better yet to have two. After the fire on the sofa, I made sure we had several in the house. You do have working smoke detectors and check them regularly, don't you?

Note: If you have been the victim of a crime such as assault, you may be able to claim some compensation through your local court. Ask at your district attorney's office as you may be able to get reimbursement for the cost of the locks etc.

Windows:

I installed heavy curtains or blinds at the windows, especially on the windows overlooking the street. I make sure these are pulled as soon as it becomes dark and before I switch on any lights. I never ever go to the window without the drapes are drawn, especially if there is a light on in the room.

Lights:

I have interior lights on a time switch so that I never enter a dark house and it also appears as though someone is home. I do the same with a radio or TV and have it go on and off at random times.

Surveillance:

As I had already purchased a surveillance system to see what Jeanette was doing here in my absence, I exchanged the spy cameras for outdoor ones, and positioned them at strategic places round the house. This was how I saw and proved to a court that she was indeed stalking me. I bought day/night cameras and have never regretted paying the extra money. These cams pick up things in the dark that even I could not see if I was outside. I was even able to help neighbors when they had a fire at their home, and my cameras could watch their house also. Depending on where you site the cameras and the monitor, you can easily see who is outside before you open the door.

Outdoor Lighting.

Outdoor lighting with motion detectors: I installed outdoor lighting with motion detectors. I have one set on my side gate with the camera positioned so that it 'sees' the gate and picks up any movement with either the light on or off.

I have others round my house including one directly over the front door and steps, thus if anyone comes to the door in the dark, I get advanced warning. I can then look at the camera for that area of the house before I open the door.

Gates:

I installed locks on all gates to my yard and where it was not possible to put locks I used chains and heavy duty padlocks. I also have a large security light in the backyard which comes on at dusk and off at dawn.

Driving:

When driving I make sure my car doors are locked at all times. I carry pepper spray in my car and also in my purse. Pepper sprays vary in effectiveness so do your homework and get a good quality spray. Pepper sprays are rated by SHU's (Scoville Heat Units). There are many good sprays on the market but there are also some poor ones. I suggest that you buy from a reputable business, even if it costs a little more. This is not the time to get a cheapo-made-abroad version! If you have to use a pepper spray, then you want it to work and also to keep the attacker as far away from you as possible. Look for a spray that goes at least 10 – 15 feet if possible. It is a good idea to have a small spray in your pocket or on a key ring and another larger one in your car.

If you have a garage for your vehicle, be sure to drive in, turn off the engine and close the door with the remote before you unlock the doors and get out. Another thing to remember is that when you walk to your car from a store, your work-place or a friend's house, check before you approach the car. Try and make sure there is no one in the back seat. Get in quickly and lock the doors immediately. Do not sit and brush your hair, write a shopping list or anything else that delays you leaving. This is asking for trouble from any crook out there and not just your abuser.

House:

I cut back the bushes that were close to my house, especially near the front entrance. I keep a small low voltage light on at the front steps all the time. I check outside with the cameras before I go out or use a door peephole. Do remember though that the peephole, if you have one, only gives a limited view of who is out there. Someone standing to the side or crouched down cannot be seen.

Handgun:

Finally I went and got my concealed carry permit for a hand gun and I carry my gun all the time when I am out at night, and in the day depending on where I am going. I know this sounds a bit like overkill, but as I have a woman stalking me who is a known drug addict, and who has threatened to shoot me, and who owns at least two large caliber handguns and a couple of rifles with scopes, I felt justified in doing the best thing I could to protect myself.

I also took classes at the local range where the police and sheriff's deputies are trained. I got good support and help, plus the local sheriff's know I have a concealed carry permit.

Am I suggesting that you buy a gun? No, not necessarily. I added this to share what I have done but this may not feel right to you. I do encourage you to get a pepper spray though, better yet get two or three.

Self Defense:

You might also look into some self defense classes, many are especially for women. Many Community Colleges run classes and they can be very helpful. I took a class years ago and learned that most women can get away from an opponent if they know what to do. Women are not expected to 'play rough' so we get the unspoken message that we are unable to protect ourselves. This is garbage, as we are well able to defend ourselves pretty well when we have been taught some tricks. It will make you feel better just to know what you can do if someone jumps you.

Your children too might benefit from similar classes or a chance to do one of the martial arts. They are great confidence builders and it gives the kids a good grounding in control as well as building strength and skill.

Surveillance Cameras

I have mentioned cameras and surveillance equipment several times throughout this book. This is a brief overview of what I learned about cameras and spy or nanny cams as they are sometimes called.

When I started thinking about being able to watch what Jeanette was doing in my absence, I knew nothing whatever about cameras and security systems. I did a lot of hunting on websites but found a lot of information regarding things I could not understand.

What I did learn was that there are basically two types of cameras or systems. One is for actual surveillance like you see in your local grocery store. The cameras are in plain view, often pointing in different directions, or they can look like a black upside down dome on the ceiling. These are the type of systems that watch for shoplifters. They are obvious to anyone walking in and have been used to watch for thieves and bank robbers etc.

The other type of system is a much more covert or hidden system. These are often called spy cams or nanny cams. These are tiny cameras hidden in everyday things so as not to be readily seen. They can be purchased already hidden in objects such as clocks, toys, DVD players and even pens and tissue boxes. There is a problem with this type of cam. They are expensive; often several hundred dollars for one unit, and they only cover a small area. To be able to see what is going on in different places in the house you would need several of these.

There are also some other really simple camera systems which do not record anything but do allow you to view who is outside. Some small units come with two cameras and a small monitor. You can also connect your TV to many simple cameras via the RCA connectors. Those are the colored connectors that are often used for VCR's and DVD players.

The other way to use spy cams is to buy a base recording unit and small cameras which you can hide yourself. The cameras themselves are only about one inch square, so are fairly easy to hide. This might seem expensive to begin with but these cameras are easily switched to surveillance cameras if or when you no longer need the spy cams.

Almost all good cameras come with a standard connector called a BNC connector. This means that almost any camera you buy will be able to connect to the main unit. The base unit will have a hard drive to record what the cameras capture, and a way for you to connect it to a

TV screen to view it. Depending on the size of the hard drive and the number of cameras you have, it can record for a couple of days to a week or more. Some are more complex and you can view the cameras remotely from any computer. This would be useful if you are at work and want to see what is happening at your house.

Because I did not know what to look for, and the nanny cams were too expensive, I went to a private detective who also specialized in surveillance equipment. I probably paid more than I needed to for used equipment but I did get a load of free help and advice about setting up the system. Mine could run four cameras, and I got three spy cams with cables that went to the base unit.

I also got a wireless one, although I was warned that they did not always work as well due to interference. I then had to decide where to locate the cams and this was the hardest part. I did not want Jeanette to see them or know what I was doing. I should also mention that it is usually legal to video anyone in any public room or in the street. It is not legal to use audio nor can you put cams in bathrooms or bedrooms or any other place where a person would expect to have privacy.

As I first wanted to see who came to the house I hid one camera in a metal jar on a windowsill. Another went into a small hole in the ceiling which I accessed from the attic. I placed four cameras in all, which gave me a good overview of the house. Once Jeanette had left the house for good, I bought outdoor day/night vision cameras and placed these round my house. I have since upgraded to an 8 camera system.

Is there hope?

I have painted a pretty dark picture of living with an addict, taken from my own experience. Many people have asked me if there is any hope that the addict may change. Just because, in my case, she refused to change does not mean that change is not possible. The magic key or vital ingredient here is that the addict themselves wants to change.

I am also often asked "What can I do to make them stop using drugs?" The answer to this one is simple. There is nothing you can do or make them do. You can offer or suggest ways for them to be able to stop, but making them is not a possibility. Even users who spend weeks in expensive rehabs often return to their drug habit at some later time. Just as with an ex-alcoholic, who is one drink away from alcoholism, the ex-user is just one snort or one hit away from their previous addiction.

Love is not enough to stop a person from using drugs. I have families tell me that they thought they just needed to love the person more. Loving is fine but do not let love turn into enabling. Drug users are people users too. They will suck you dry and look for more. More ways to get their drugs.

There are drug users who have been long time users who manage to get clean and stay that way. One of my closest friends, whom I originally met through my work with addicts, was a heroin user for over 20 years. Now in her mid 40's she has been clean for at least 5 years. She was determined to stay off the drugs that killed so many of her friends and family. However both she and I know that she could relapse into drug use again at any time. Once a person has been addicted, they need to be vigilant for the rest of their life.

What does this mean for you? Only you can be the judge. Be aware of the dangers of living with a user and do your best to mitigate the damage that the drugs can do to you and other innocent family members. Leave if you need to, or get them to leave. The leaving may not be permanent but this will depend on the user. You cannot control what he or she does but you do have control over what you do. At some time you may be able to live in the same house again. It is possible that the separation will give the user reason to get clean. However, this is not a given.

Afterword from Vivienne

Have I covered every possible danger? Probably not! Why? Because drug addicts are in inventive lot and whenever you think you have seen it all, they throw you a curved ball. I hope though, that I have given you some things to think about and some suggestions to be safe.

You cannot change what the drug addict does but you can change what you do. After Jeanette was gone I realized how much I had learned about drug addiction. I also realized that I had little in the way of guidance while dealing with her. Most of the focus via the Internet is on the user, not the family. That is why I developed my website, http://www.drug-addiction-family-recovery.com. If you would like to learn more about me and how I help the families of addicts, please go to my website.

If you would like to see actual pictures of my house after Jeanette left, please go to http://youtu.be/ru5iiZFnxzc

Would you rate this book for me please? I have enjoyed writing it and I would love some feedback. If you feel it has been helpful, maybe others would find it helpful too. Remember you cannot force change on an addict, you can only change what you yourself can do. Above all, be safe.

About the Author

Vivienne Gardner Edwards grew up in England. She finished her education in Oxford and moved with her family to Michigan in the mid 70's. She later moved to Minnesota where she was active in Home Education and she created a state home school network in the 80's.

After she moved to Oregon she became a speaker on domestic abuse until she became concerned over drug abuse after sharing her home with a heavy drug user. She formed a local area drug education network, working with local law enforcement and schools to educate others about drugs and their effects on both the user and the family.

Two years later, she wanted to expand the reach of this work so she created an educational website dedicated to the support of families of drug users. Realizing the need for support for Veterans, who often deal with addiction to pain medication, she provides specific support for Veterans. For drug information please visit www.drug-addiction-family-recovery.com.

As well as working on drug related issues, she also writes fiction books and is currently working on a book on PTSD for Veterans. Details of all her books can be found at her personal website, www.vivienne-gardner-edwards.com.

Made in the USA
San Bernardino, CA
22 January 2014